The Ultimate Self-Teaching Method!

Play Guitar Today! Songbook

Featuring 10 Rock & Pop Favorites!

PLAYBACK+
Speed • Pitch • Balance • Loop

To access audio visit:
www.halleonard.com/mylibrary

8694-7758-8283-9840

Recording Credits:
Todd Greene & Rich Plath, Vocals
Scott Schroedl, Drums
Doug Boduch, Guitar
Tom McGirr, Bass
Jake Johnson, Engineer
Recorded at Sleepless Nights Recording Studios, Madison, WI

ISBN 978-0-634-00411-7

7777 W. BLUEMOUND RD. P.O. BOX 13819 MILWAUKEE, WI 53213

For all works contained herein:
Unauthorized copying, arranging, adapting, recording, Internet posting, public performance, or other distribution
of the printed or recorded music in this publication is an infringement of copyright.
Infringers are liable under the law.

Visit Hal Leonard Online at
www.halleonard.com

Introduction

Welcome to the *Guitar Songbook*. This book includes several well-known rock and pop favorites, and is intended for the beginner to intermediate player.

The ten songs in this book are carefully coordinated with the skills introduced throughout levels one and two of the method, *Play Guitar Today!* Refer to the right column in the table of contents below to know when you're ready to play each piece.

Contents

About the Audio

A full-band recording of each song in the book is included, so you can hear how it sounds and play along when you're ready. Each example is preceded by one measure of "clicks" to indicate the tempo and meter. Pan right to hear the guitar part emphasized. Pan left to hear the accompaniment emphasized.

Before you begin, tune your guitar to the tuning notes on track 1.

Song Structure

Most songs have different sections, that might be recognizable by any or all of the following:

- **Introduction** (or "Intro"): This is a short section at the beginning that "introduces" the song to the listeners.
- **Verses**: One of the main sections of the song—the part that includes most of the storyline—is the *verse*. There will usually be several verses, all with the same music but each with different lyrics.
- **Chorus**: Perhaps the most memorable section of the song is the *chorus*. Again, there might be several choruses, but each chorus will often have the same lyrics and music.
- **Bridge**: This section makes a transition from one part of a song to the next. For example, you may find a bridge between the chorus and next verse.
- **Solos**: Sometimes solos are played over the verse or chorus structure, but in some songs the solo section has its own structure. This is your time to shine!
- **Outro**: Similar to the "intro," this section brings the song to an end.

Lyrics

All of the lyrics to all of the great songs in this book are included. They are shown above the staff in italics as a guide to help you keep your place in the music.

Endings

Several of the songs have some new symbols that you must understand before playing. Each of these symbols represents a different type of ending.

First and Second Endings

Play the song through to the first ending, repeat back to the first repeat sign, or beginning of the song (whichever is the case). Play through the song again, but skip the first ending and play the second ending.

D.S. al Coda

When you see these words, go back and repeat from this symbol: 𝄋

Play until you see the words "To Coda," then skip to the Coda, indicated by this symbol: 𝄌

Now just finish the song.

Let It Be

Words and Music by John Lennon and Paul McCartney

Copyright © 1970 Sony/ATV Songs LLC
Copyright Renewed
All Rights Administered by Sony/ATV Music Publishing, 8 Music Square West, Nashville, TN 37203
International Copyright Secured   All Rights Reserved

Additional Lyrics

2. And when the broken hearted people
   Living in the world agree,
   There will be an answer, let it be.
   For tho' they may be parted
   There is still a chance that they will see,
   There will be an answer, let it be.

3. And when the night is cloudy
   There is still a light that shines on me,
   Shine until tomorrow, let it be.
   I wake up to the sound of music
   Mother Mary comes to me,
   Speaking words of wisdom, let it be.

Brown Eyed Girl
Words and Music by Van Morrison

Copyright © 1967 Songs Of PolyGram International, Inc.
Copyright Renewed
International Copyright Secured   All Rights Reserved

Additional Lyrics

2. Whatever happened to Tuesday and so slow,
   Going down the old mine with a transistor radio?
   Standing in the sunlight laughing,
   Hiding behind a rainbow's wall,
   Slipping and a-sliding
   All along the waterfall
   With you, my brown eyed girl.
   You, my brown eyed girl.
   Do you remember when we used to sing;

3. So hard to find my way, now that I'm all on my own.
   I saw you just the other day, my, how you have grown.
   Cast my memory back there, Lord,
   Sometimes I'm overcome thinking 'bout it.
   Making love in the green grass
   Behind the stadium
   With you, my brown eyed girl.
   You, my brown eyed girl.
   Do you remember when we used to sing;

Every Breath You Take

Written and Composed by Sting

© 1983 G.M. SUMNER
Published by MAGNETIC PUBLISHING LTD. and Administered by EMI BLACKWOOD MUSIC INC. in the USA and Canada
All Rights Reserved   International Copyright Secured   Used by Permission

Additional Lyrics

2. Ev'ry single day, ev'ry word you say,
   Ev'ry game you play, ev'ry night you stay,
   I'll be watching you.

Time Is on My Side

Words and Music by Jerry Ragovoy

Intro
Moderately ♩ = 74
(organ)

Chorus

Time ... is on my side. Yes, it is. Time is on my side. Yes, it is.

Verse

1. Now, you always say that you wanna be free. But you come runnin' back. You said you would, baby.

2., 3. See Additional Lyrics

You come runnin' back. You said so many times before. You come runnin' back to me. Oh.

To Coda ⊕

Copyright © 1999 by HAL LEONARD CORPORATION
International Copyright Secured   All Rights Reserved

Additional Lyrics

2. You're searchin' for good times, but just wait and see.
   You'll come runnin' back; I won't have to worry no more.
   You'll come runnin' back; spend the rest of my life with you, babe.
   You'll come runnin' back to me.

3. 'Cause I got the real love, the kind that you need.
   You'll come runnin' back; you said you would, baby.
   You'll come runnin' back; like I always said you would.
   You'll come runnin' back to me.

Wild Thing

Words and Music by Chip Taylor

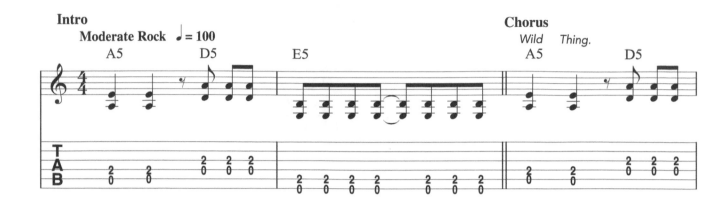

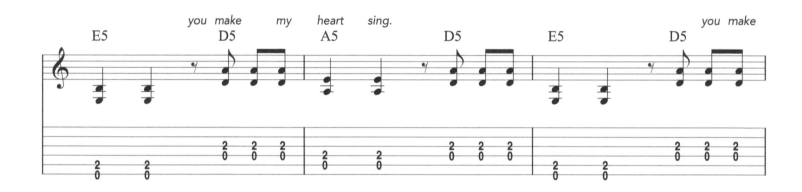

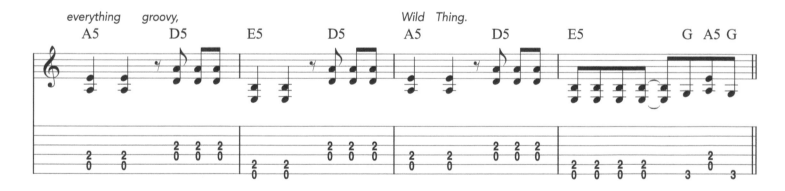

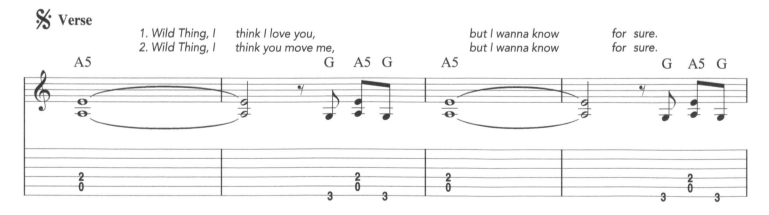

© 1965 (Renewed 1993) EMI BLACKWOOD MUSIC INC.
All Rights Reserved   International Copyright Secured   Used by Permission

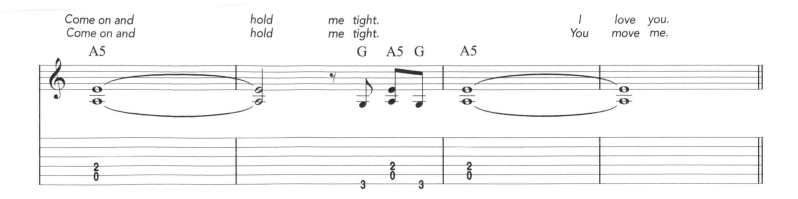

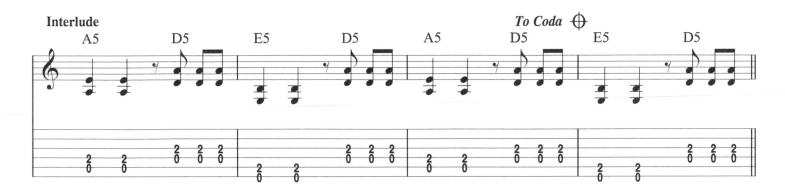

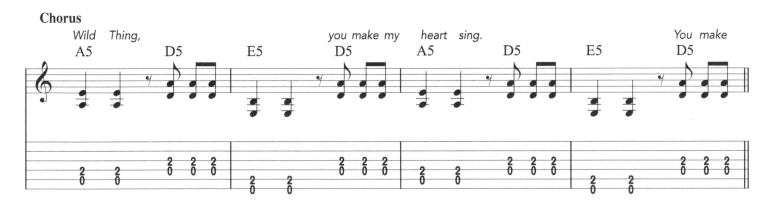

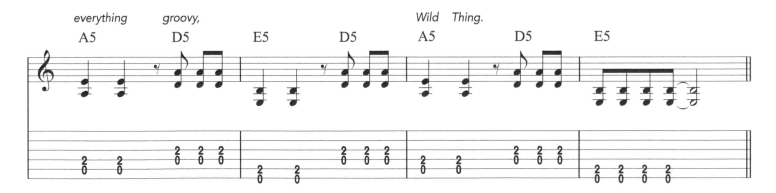

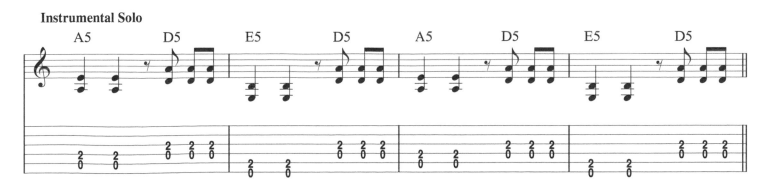

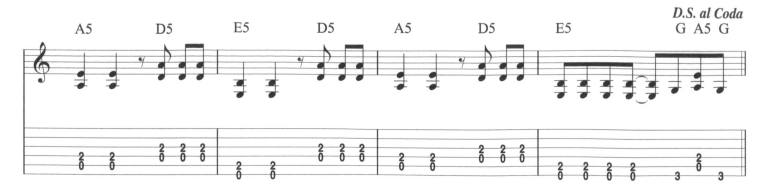

Coda

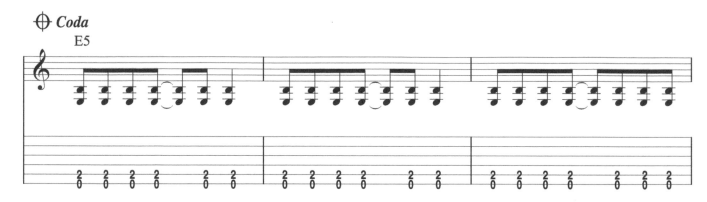

Outro-Chorus

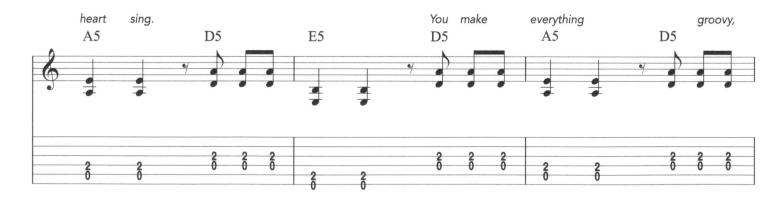

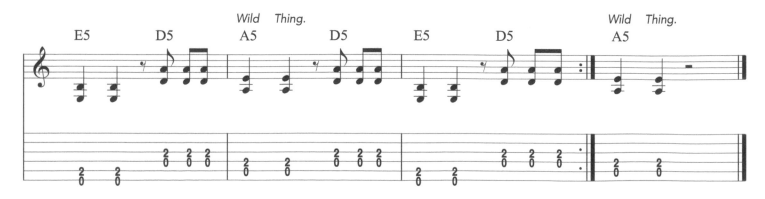

(blank page to facilitate page turn)

You Really Got Me

Words and Music by Ray Davies

Intro
Moderate Rock ♩ = 130

%. **Verse**

1. Girl,   you really   got me goin'.   You got me
2. See,   don't ever   set me free.   I always

so   I don't know what I'm doin'.   Yeah,   you   really
wanna   be by your side.   Girl,   you   really

got me now. You   got me   so I can't sleep at night.

Yeah,   you really   got me now. You got me   so I don't know what I'm doin'.   Oh,

Copyright © 1964 Jayboy Music Corp.
Copyright Renewed
All Rights Administered by Sony/ATV Music Publishing, 8 Music Square West, Nashville, TN 37203
International Copyright Secured   All Rights Reserved

Oh, Pretty Woman

Words and Music by Roy Orbison and Bill Dees

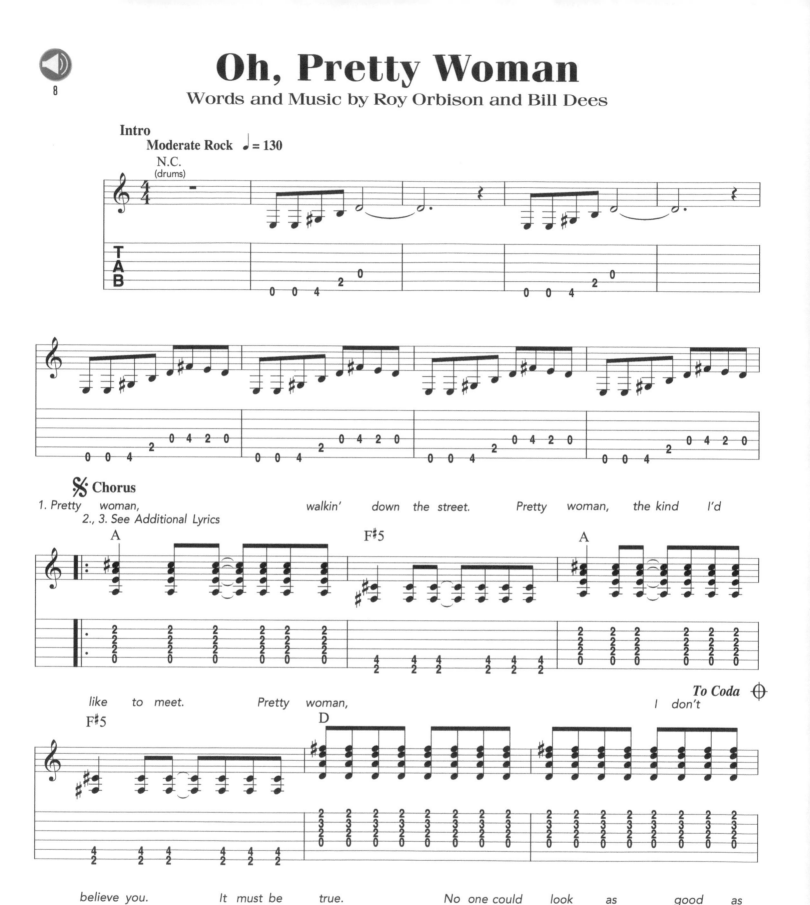

Intro
Moderate Rock ♩ = 130

Chorus

1. Pretty woman, walkin' down the street. Pretty woman, the kind I'd
2., 3. See Additional Lyrics

like to meet. Pretty woman, I don't

To Coda ⊕

believe you. It must be true. No one could look as good as

Copyright © 1964 (Renewed 1992) Acuff-Rose Music, Inc., Barbara Orbison Music Company,
Orbi-Lee Music and R-Key Darkus Music
All Rights Reserved   Used by Permission

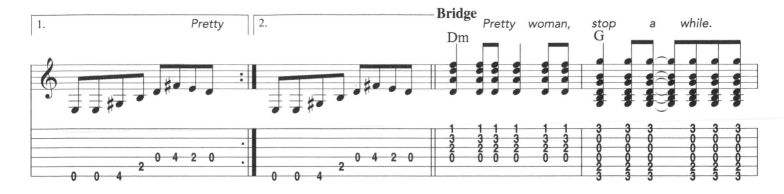

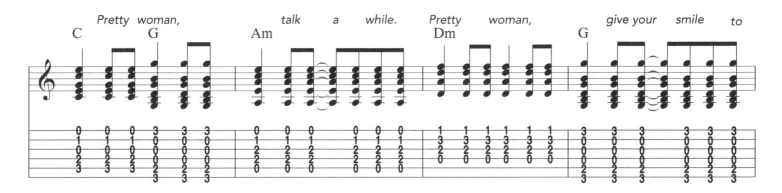

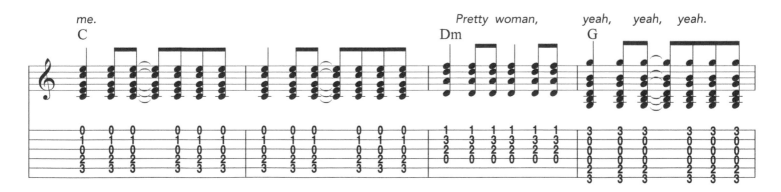

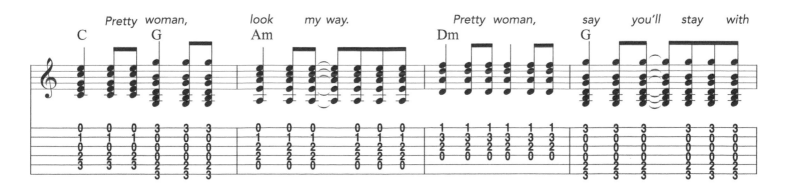

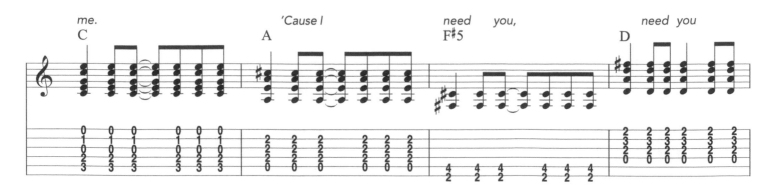

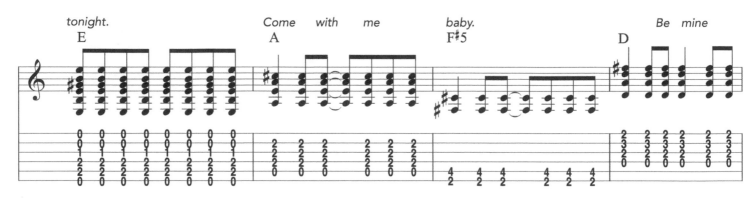

D.S. al Coda
3. Pretty

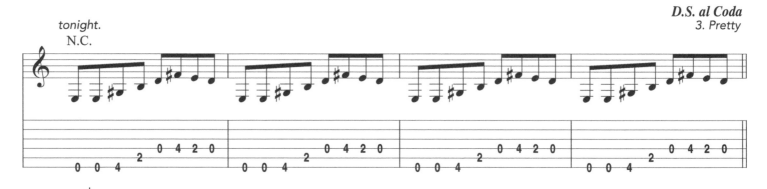

⊕ *Coda*

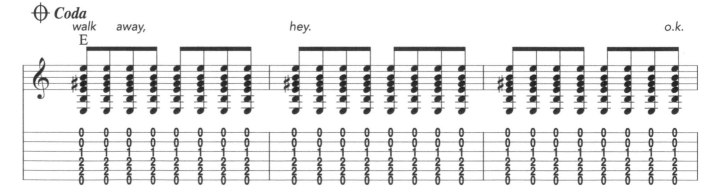

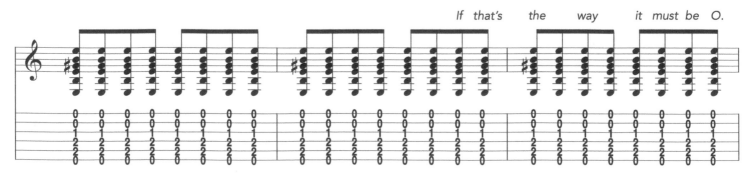

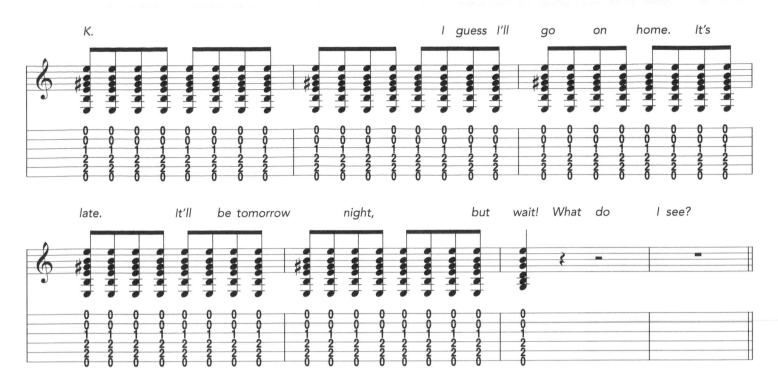

K.

I guess I'll go on home. It's

late. It'll be tomorrow night, but wait! What do I see?

Outro

N.C.

Is she walking back to me?

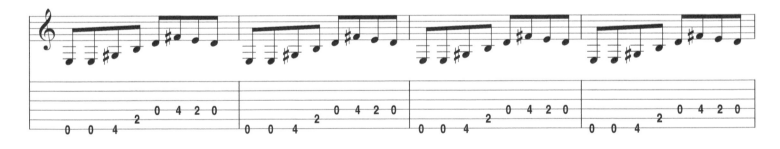

Whoa, whoa, pretty woman.

A5

Additional Lyrics

2. Pretty woman, won't you pardon me?
   Pretty woman, I couldn't help but see;
   Pretty woman, that you look lovely as can be.
   Are you lonely just like me?

3. Pretty woman, don't walk on by.
   Pretty woman, don't make me cry.
   Pretty woman, don't walk away, hey...

American Pie

Words and Music by Don McLean

© Copyright 1971, 1972 by MUSIC CORPORATION OF AMERICA, INC. and THE BENNY BIRD CO. INC.
All Rights Controlled and Administered by MUSIC CORPORATION OF AMERICA, INC.
International Copyright Secured   All Rights Reserved
MCA Music Publishing

how   to   dance   real   slow?   Well,   I

A7   **D7**

know   that   you're   in   love   with   him, 'cause I   saw   you   dancin'

Em   **D**   **Em**

in   the   gym.   You   both   kicked   off your   shoes.   Man,   I

D7   **C**   **G**   **Am**

dig   those   rhythm and blues.   I was a   lonely   teenage

C   **D7**   **G**   **D**

broncin'   buck   with   a   pink carnation an'   a   pickup   truck.   But

Em   **Am**   **C**

I   knew   I   was   out   of   luck,   the   day   the

G   **D**   **Em**   **C**

music   died.   I   started singin',

D7   **G**   **C**   **G**   **D**

Chorus

"Bye,   Bye,   Miss   American   Pie.   Drove   my   Chevy to the levee, but the

G   **C**   **G**   **D**   **G**   **C**

levee was dry. Them good ol' boys were drinkin' whiskey an' rye, an singin',

G D G C G D

"This'll be the day that I die, this'll be the day that I

Em A7 Em

die." 1., 2., 3. 4. D.S. al Coda

D7

✛ Coda
Outro-Chorus

"Bye, bye Miss American Pie. Drove my Chevy to the levee but the levee was dry. Them

G C G D G C G D

good ol' boys were drinkin' whiskey an' rye, singing; "This'll be the day that I die."

G C G D C D G C G

Additional Lyrics

2. Now for ten years we've been on our own, an' moss grows
    fat on a rolling stone.
But, that's not how it used to be.
When the jester sang for the king an' queen in a coat he
    borrowed from James Dean.
An' a voice that came from you and me.
Oh, an' while the king was looking down, the jester stole his
    thorny crown.
The courtroom was adjourned; no verdict was returned.
And while Lenin read a book on Marx, a quartet practiced
    in the park.
And we sang dirges in the dark, the day the music died.
    We started singin'…

3. Helter, skelter in the summer swelter.
The birds flew off for the fallout shelter, eight miles high
    an' fallin' fast.
It landed foul out on the grass.
The players tried for a forward pass, with the jester on the
    sidelines in a cast.
Now, the halftime air was sweet perfume, while the
    sergeants played a marchin' tune.
We all got up to dance, oh, but we never got the chance.
'Cause the players tried to take the field, the marching band
    refused to yield.
Do you recall what was revealed the day the music died?
    We started singin'…

4. Oh, an' there we were all in one place;
    A generation lost in space, with no time left to start again.
    So, come on, Jack be nimble, Jack be quick,
    Jack Flash sat on a candle stick, 'cause fire is the devil's only friend.
    Oh, and as I watched him on the stage my hands were clenched in fists of rage.
    No angel born in Hell could break that Satan's spell.
    And as the flames climbed high into the night to light the sacrificial rite,
    I saw Satan laughing with delight, the day the music died? He was singing'…

Born to Be Wild

Words and Music by Mars Bonfire

© Copyright 1968 by MANITOU MUSIC CANADA, A Division of MCA CANADA LTD.
Copyright Renewed
All Rights for the USA Controlled and Administered by MUSIC CORPORATION OF AMERICA, INC.
International Copyright Secured   All Rights Reserved

MCA Music Publishing

and whatever comes our way.
and the feelin' that I'm under.

Yeah, darlin' gonna make it happen.   Take the world in a

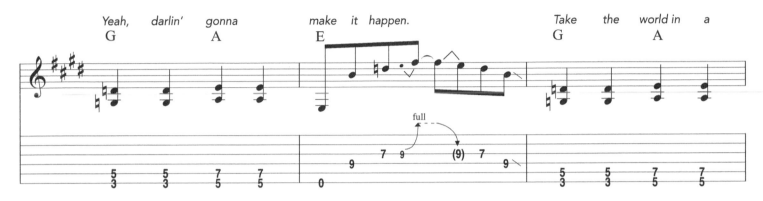

love embrace.   Fire all of your guns at once and   explode into

space.   space. Like a true nature's child   we were

born,   born to be wild.   We can climb so high.   I never wanna

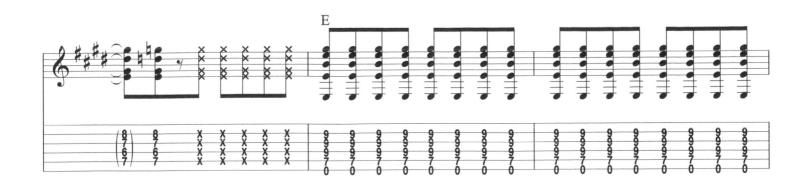

D.S. al Coda
(take 2nd ending)

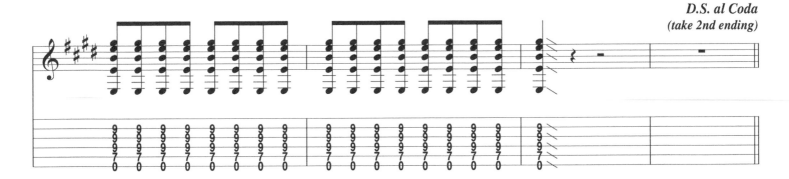

⊕ *Coda*
Outro

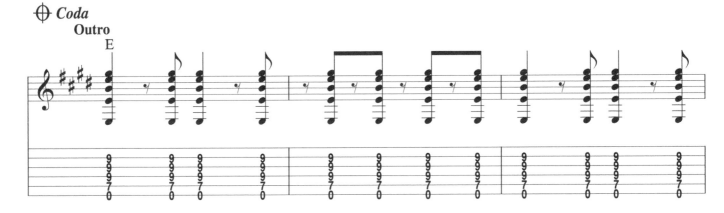

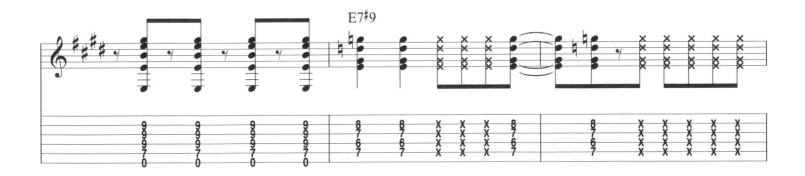

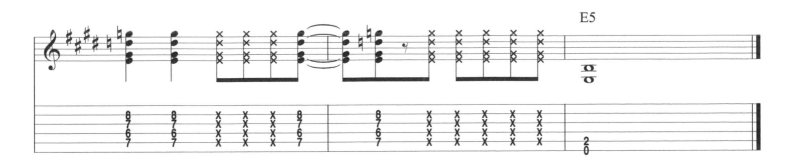

I Shot the Sheriff

Words and Music by Bob Marley

Copyright © 1974 Fifty-Six Hope Road Music Ltd. and Odnil Music Ltd.
All Rights for the United States and Canada Administered by PolyGram International Publishing, Inc.
International Copyright Secured   All Rights Reserved

bring me in guilty

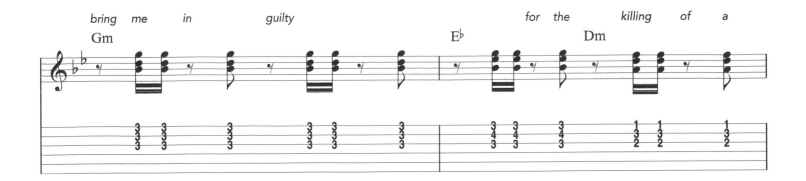

for the killing of a

deputy,   for the   life   of   the deputy.   But   I   say…

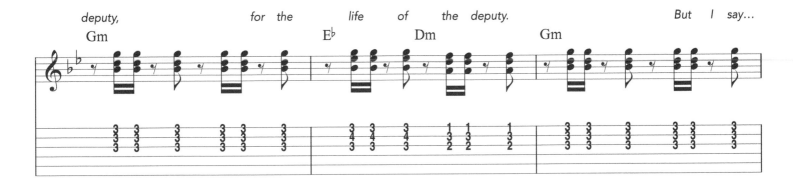

Additional Lyrics

2. Sheriff John Brown always hated me;
   For what I did I don't know.
   And every time I try to plant that little seed,
   He said, "Kill it before it grows,"
   "Kill it before it grows."

3. Freedom came my way one fine day,
   So I headed straight out of town.
   All of a sudden, I see Sheriff John Brown
   Aimin' to shoot me down,
   So I shot I shot him down.

4. Reflexes got the better of me,
   What will be will be.
   Everytime the bucket goes to the well,
   One day the bottom will drop out
   One day the bottom will drop out.

Play Today! Series
The Ultimate Self-Teaching Series

These are complete guides to the basics, designed to offer quality instruction, terrific songs, and professional-quality audio with tons of full-demo tracks and instruction. Each book includes over 70 great songs and examples!

Play Accordion Today!
00701744	Level 1 Book/Audio	$10.99
00702657	Level 1 Songbook Book/Audio	$12.99

Play Alto Sax Today!
00842049	Level 1 Book/Audio	$9.99
00842050	Level 2 Book/Audio	$9.99
00320359	DVD	$14.95
00842051	Songbook Book/Audio	$12.95
00699555	Beginner's – Level 1 Book/Audio & DVD	$19.95
00699492	Play Today Plus Book/Audio	$14.95

Play Banjo Today!
00699897	Level 1 Book/Audio	$9.99
00701006	Level 2 Book/Audio	$9.99
00320913	DVD	$14.99
00115999	Songbook Book/Audio	$12.99
00701873	Beginner's – Level 1 Book/Audio & DVD	$19.95

Play Bass Today!
00842020	Level 1 Book/Audio	$9.99
00842036	Level 2 Book/Audio	$9.99
00320356	DVD	$14.95
00842037	Songbook Book/Audio	$12.95
00699552	Beginner's – Level 1 Book/Audio & DVD	$19.99

Play Cello Today!
00151353	Level 1 Book/Audio	$9.99

Play Clarinet Today!
00842046	Level 1 Book/Audio	$9.99
00842047	Level 2 Book/Audio	$9.99
00320358	DVD	$14.95
00842048	Songbook Book/Audio	$12.95
00699554	Beginner's – Level 1 Book/Audio & DVD	$19.95
00699490	Play Today Plus Book/Audio	$14.95

Play Dobro Today!
00701505	Level 1 Book/Audio	$9.99

Play Drums Today!
00842021	Level 1 Book/Audio	$9.99
00842038	Level 2 Book/Audio	$9.95
00320355	DVD	$14.95
00842039	Songbook Book/Audio	$12.95
00699551	Beginner's – Level 1 Book/Audio & DVD	$19.95
00703291	Starter	$24.99

Play Flute Today
00842043	Level 1 Book/Audio	$9.95
00842044	Level 2 Book/Audio	$9.99
00320360	DVD	$14.95
00842045	Songbook Book/Audio	$12.95
00699553	Beginner's – Level 1 Book/Audio & DVD	$19.95

Play Guitar Today!
00696100	Level 1 Book/Audio	$9.99
00696101	Level 2 Book/Audio	$9.99
00320353	DVD	$14.95
00696102	Songbook Book/Audio	$12.99
00699544	Beginner's – Level 1 Book/Audio & DVD	$19.95
00702431	Worship Songbook Book/Audio	$12.99
00695662	Complete Kit	$29.95

Play Harmonica Today!
00700179	Level 1 Book/Audio	$9.99
00320653	DVD	$14.99
00701875	Beginner's – Level 1 Book/Audio & DVD	$19.95

Play Mandolin Today!
00699911	Level 1 Book/Audio	$9.99
00320909	DVD	$14.99
00115029	Songbook Book/Audio	$12.99
00701874	Beginner's – Level 1 Book/Audio & DVD	$19.99

Play Piano Today!
00842019	Level 1 Book/Audio	$9.99
00842040	Level 2 Book/Audio	$9.95
00842041	Songbook Book/Audio	$12.95
00699545	Beginner's – Level 1 Book/Audio & DVD	$19.95
00702415	Worship Songbook Book/Audio	$12.99
00703707	Complete Kit	$22.99

Play Recorder Today!
00700919	Level 1 Book/Audio	$7.99
00119830	Complete Kit	$19.99

Sing Today!
00699761	Level 1 Book/Audio	$10.99

Play Trombone Today!
00699917	Level 1 Book/Audio	$12.99
00320508	DVD	$14.95

Play Trumpet Today!
00842052	Level 1 Book/Audio	$9.99
00842053	Level 2 Book/Audio	$9.95
00320357	DVD	$14.95
00842054	Songbook Book/Audio	$12.95
00699556	Beginner's – Level 1 Book/Audio & DVD	$19.95

Play Ukulele Today!
00699638	Level 1 Book/Audio	$10.99
00699655	Play Today Plus Book/Audio	$9.99
00320985	DVD	$14.99
00701872	Beginner's – Level 1 Book/Audio & DVD	$19.95
00650743	Book/Audio/DVD with Ukulele	$39.99
00701002	Level 2 Book/Audio	$9.99
00702484	Level 2 Songbook Book/Audio	$12.99
00703290	Starter	$24.99

Play Viola Today!
00142679	Level 1 Book/Audio	$9.99

Play Violin Today!
00699748	Level 1 Book/Audio	$9.99
00701320	Level 2 Book/Audio	$9.99
00321076	DVD	$14.99
00701700	Songbook Book/Audio	$12.99
00701876	Beginner's – Level 1 Book/Audio & DVD	$19.95

HAL•LEONARD®

www.halleonard.com

Prices, contents and availability subject to change without notice.